PAUL
Ambassador of Peace

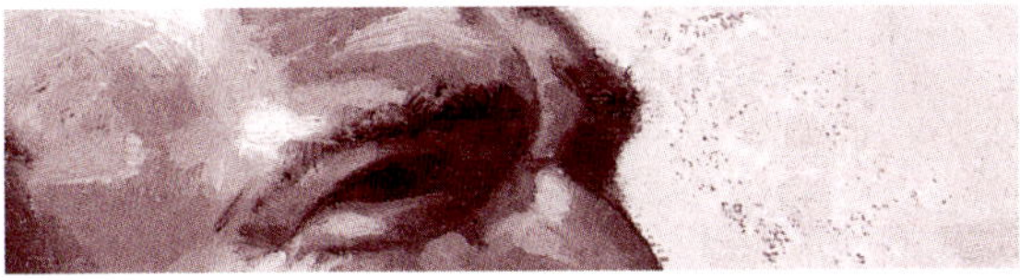

Jon D. Buchholz

NORTHWESTERN PUBLISHING HOUSE
Milwaukee, Wisconsin

In memory of my sainted grandfather, the Reverend V. H. Winter,
a disciple of Jesus who walked in the footsteps of the apostle Paul.

Cover illustration: Johnson and Fancher
Interior illustrations: Troy Allen, Samantha Burton, Frank Ordaz

Northwestern Publishing House
1250 N. 113th St., Milwaukee, WI 53226-3284
www.nph.net

Published 2004
Printed in the United States of America
ISBN 0-8100-1346-0

CONTENTS

FOREWORD

They have been referred to as the saints, the Hebrews, the Israelites, a remnant, and the church. They are God's people—his *chosen* people. They belong to him; so precious that he would go to impossible lengths to overcome the gulf that separates them from himself. You and I are among them.

The books in this series are a recital of the life and times of some of them—Noah, Jacob, Ruth, David, Jonah, Paul, and others. Their stories involve conflict and resolution, pain and tragedy, despondency and renewal. They present disturbing images from the underbelly of human depravity, and visions of untold glory that transport us to the soaring heights of ultimate conquest. The plots and settings are drawn from the living record of the Bible. Series authors and editors were careful to remain faithful to that record. But in an effort to make the text come alive, these narratives speculate occasionally to provide additional background to the story.

In these stories we see God's people wrestling with their humanity and struggling to find respite for their souls. Each story is unique in its own right. Yet two common threads run through the fabric of their stories and ours. The first is the thread of the bitter curse of sin. The second is the golden thread of salvation in Christ Jesus. We can readily identify with both, for we share these same two themes with all of God's people. Their stories, like ours, rest forever in God's abiding grace.

Kenneth Kremer, Series Editor

AMBASSADOR OF PEACE

Tarsus was already an ancient city when Saul was born. With its noisy bazaars and crowded streets, it was a melting pot of people, cultures, and ideas. Now the young Jew's heart welled up with thanksgiving and pride. The Jewish community was strong in Tarsus, and Saul was proud that the God of Israel had set him apart as a member of his chosen people. Saul's father was a member of the influential Pharisee sect. Young Saul had been brought up under strict Jewish law. At his circumcision Saul had received the name of the first king of Israel; he too had come from the tribe of Benjamin.

But Saul had not only been born and bred a Jew. By virtue of his father's citizenship, he had also come into this world as a citizen of the Roman Empire—the most powerful empire on earth. Special dispensations and distinct advantages came with citizenship. The gentile Romans—with whom Saul had no more contact than was necessary—called the young man by his Latin name Paulus, or Paul.

What promise the young intellectual's life held! With thanksgiving in his heart and a psalm of praise on his lips, Saul renewed his commitment to serve the God of Israel. Yet even he could not have imagined either the scope or the importance of the divine mission outlined for him in eternity. One day the God of Abraham, Isaac, and Jacob would call on this brilliant young man to change the course of history. Then Saul of Tarsus would be known and acclaimed the world over and to future generations as Paul, an apostle of Christ and the Almighty's great missionary at large.

Map of Paul's Life

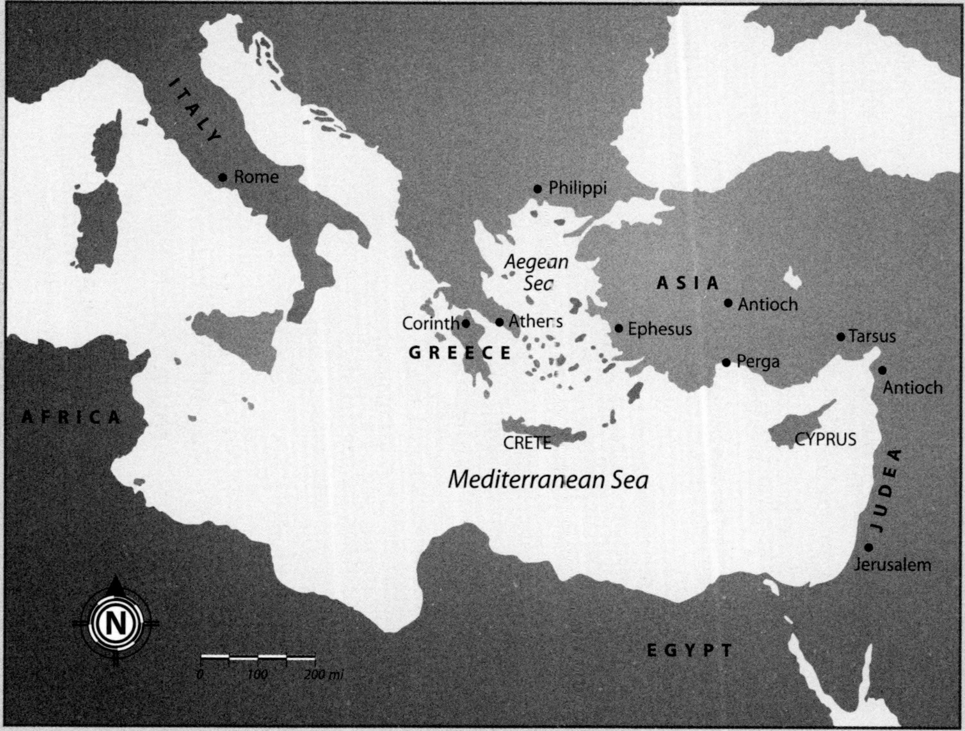

1 THE RIGORS OF APOSTLESHIP

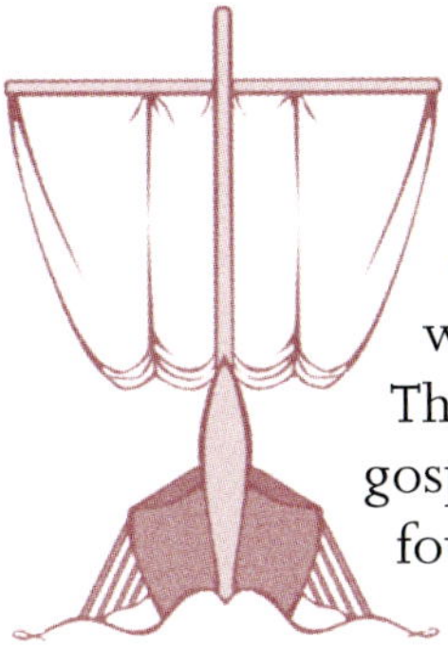

Paul stoked the fire. The flames flared, and for a moment they drove back the creeping chill of the Macedonian air. He sighed. It wasn't just the late autumn air that was cold. The attitude of the Macedonians toward the gospel was downright frigid. The apostle again found himself ridiculed and persecuted by the enemies of Christ.

The firelight illuminated a face that was worn and tired. Its deep creases told of the rigors of apostleship. Paul's body was weak. He wrestled with a persistent ailment—his thorn in the flesh. Now, in the autumn of his life, Paul's compulsion to preach Christ to the Gentiles drove him to exhaustion.

This was a difficult time. The divisions in the congregation at Corinth still hadn't healed. In Philippi, Ephesus, the towns of Galatia, and in places Paul had not yet visited, the gospel was only beginning to pierce the pagan darkness. To human eyes the future of the fledgling church seemed anything but certain. The weary apostle poured out his soul in prayer and found strength in the promises of his Master, Jesus.

From Macedonia, Paul drafted yet another letter to the divisive Corinthians. He urged them to remember their high calling and encouraged them to persevere. He recalled his own sufferings for the gospel. "I have worked much harder, been in prison more frequently, been flogged more severely, and been exposed to death again and again. Five times I received from the Jews the forty lashes minus one. Three times I was beaten with rods, once I was stoned, three times I was shipwrecked, I spent a night and a day in the open sea. I have been constantly on the move. I have been in danger from bandits, in danger from my own countrymen, in danger from Gentiles; in danger in the city, in danger in the country, in danger at sea; and in danger from false brothers. I have labored and toiled and have often gone without sleep; I have known hunger and thirst and have often gone without food; I have been cold and naked. Besides everything else, I face daily the pressure of my concern for all the churches."

The apostle had known a hard life. He enjoyed few material comforts. His body bore the marks of violence. But Paul expected nothing less. His life belonged to Christ and to no one else. It made no difference where he preached; his true citizenship was above. No matter what violence he encountered, no matter what opposition he faced, his resolve remained the same—steadfast and firm. He was an ambassador of peace.

A RELIGIOUS ZEALOT 2

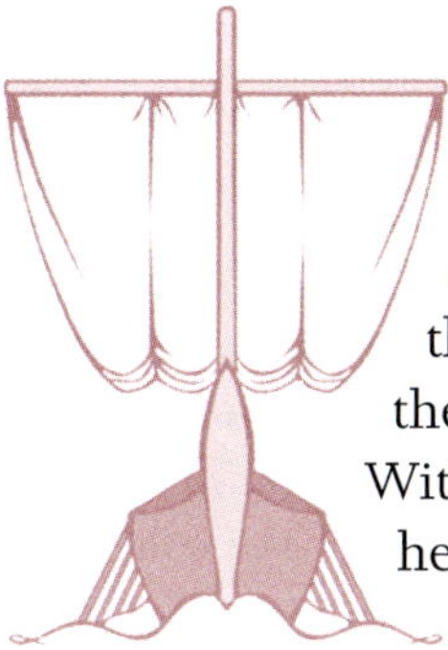

Jerusalem was magnificent. The temple, built by Herod the Great, crowned the city. It was a beacon inviting weary travelers to worship the one true God. Visitors paused and fell on their knees at the sight. Some wept openly. With outstretched arms and eyes uplifted toward heaven, they praised God for safe journeys to the Holy City.

Saul had come to Jerusalem to study. Rabbi Gamaliel was the most respected Jewish teacher of the day. Saul's father's influence had won Saul a place at the great rabbi's feet. As Saul immersed himself in the traditions of his forefathers, the young disciple matured into a zealous disciple of the Torah. He measured himself against the commandments. And he imagined God's pleasure with his obedience. "I am not only a Jew," he congratulated himself. "I am a Pharisee—and a good one at that."

But even in Jerusalem, at the center of the Jewish faith, Saul saw problems. It troubled him that some Jews could take their God for granted. Saul had witnessed the foolishness of pagan religions. He had seen firsthand the folly of Greek philosophy. The cult of Mithraism—a religious import from Persia—was strong in Tarsus. These fanatics imagined themselves cleansed from evil as they bathed in the blood of a slain bull. Such rituals made Saul's skin crawl. "How wicked! Disgusting!" he shuddered. The Mithraic cult had no more value than the Greek philosophy of stoicism, which said life was only to be endured. Or Epicureanism, which said, "Eat, drink, and be merry, for tomorrow we die!" "Empty and useless!" thought Saul. Yes, it was good to be a Jew. "How could so many of my fellow Jews not understand what we've been given?" he wondered. His heart filled with contempt as he thought of his Jewish countrymen who did not share his passion. They were casual toward the Torah. They were lax in obeying the commandments. And they fraternized with unclean Gentiles.

Christianity's rise in Jerusalem

Saul's fellow Pharisees had toasted the demise of Jesus of Nazareth, cheering the miracle worker's painful death on a Roman cross. Now they were hoping for a speedy end to this messianic movement. Rumors of Jesus' resurrection were little cause for concern; the soldiers at the tomb had been paid well. In response they circulated the story that some of Jesus' disciples had spirited the corpse away. Saul and his friends were naively unaware that they were facing a force that went beyond their wildest imaginations.

Then, 50 days after the Passover, at Pentecost, when Jews from all around the empire were once again converging on Jerusalem, God's Holy Spirit was poured out upon the ragtag remains of Jesus' followers. Tongues of fire and other spiritual signs appeared, confirming the Lord's powerful gifts for spreading the good news of a living Christ. Peter, the most outspoken of the original 12, had preached a powerful sermon. His message convicted many of the Jews of their sins and pointed them to Jesus as their only Savior. On that day three thousand people were baptized into Christ!

The Pentecost believers carried their newfound faith with them back to the lands where they lived, and the message of the cross and the resurrection quickly spread. The new Christians called themselves followers of the Way. Suddenly they were a force to be reckoned with.

Christians wore their religion on their sleeves. They met openly in the temple for prayer and fellowship. They boldly shared their love for Jesus, the Son of God. They gathered together to take part in the sacramental meal of Jesus' body and blood, claiming that God himself blesses his people with his divine forgiveness hidden in the bread and wine. It was a love feast reserved for true believers, baptized converts, alone—the number of which was growing rapidly. All Jerusalem was abuzz with the good news.

Saul the inquisitor

Saul hated Jesus. As the movement of messianic believers grew, so did the loathing in Saul's heart. "What blasphemy," he raged, "that this carpenter from Nazareth should be called the Son of God!" The mystery meal of the Christians reminded him of the cult of Mithraism—only the sacrament of the Way, which smacked to him of cannibalism, seemed worse. There was only one solution: Jesus' followers had to be exterminated.

Saul soon had his first taste of blood. A well-spoken man named Stephen dared to confront the Sanhedrin with the teachings of Jesus. Stephen was a leader among the disciples, a deacon in the new church. He accused the members of the Sanhedrin of killing the Christ—and the Jewish rulers responded with fury. They gnashed their teeth, covered their ears, yelled at the top of their voices, and dragged Stephen outside the walls of Jerusalem to stone him.

Saul gladly cast a vote for Stephen's death. Outside the city, he held the cloaks of those who hurled the stones. "Here is my cause!" he thought to himself. Saul's appetite for the blood of Christians had been whetted.

In the wake of their persecution in Jerusalem, the followers of the Way scattered into the surrounding countryside, and the message of Jesus spread throughout Judea and Samaria. Philip, another of Jesus' faithful disciples, baptized a man from Ethiopia, and the message spread south.

The spread of the messianic message infuriated Saul. He developed a systematic plan to root out and destroy Christians. He would use torture to extract confessions and throw into prison anyone who confessed Jesus as Lord. Surely, he reasoned, God would be pleased.

But Saul could enjoy no peace until his task was done completely. The inquisition had to be expanded. "Let me do the Lord's work in Damascus," Saul asked the high priest. "With your authority, we can put a stop to this movement and silence the message of Jesus forever."

"Go, my son," said the high priest. "Arrest those blasphemers in Damascus. You have my blessing!"

With righteous rage, Saul recommitted himself to stamping out this insult to his beloved traditions. But God in heaven—whom Saul thought he was serving—had a different plan.

Pharisees and Sadducees

Two sectarian groups known as the Pharisees and the Sadducees developed some time during the long silent period before Christ was born. The Hebrew root for *pharisee* means "to separate." It insinuates an attitude of physical, ritual, and spiritual superiority. The Pharisees' source of moral authority stretched beyond Mosaic Law to include a tradition of oral law. Pharisees typically influenced society at a local level, teaching (and recruiting) in the many local religious schools. They believed in angels, a bodily resurrection, and the immortality of the soul. They denounced Jesus for breaking Sabbath laws and associating with sinners.

Jesus called the Pharisees hypocrites, or bad actors, a reference to their self-righteous public obsessing over fine points of law while personally ignoring the principles of justice, mercy, and faith.

Men of compromise and statesmanship, the Sadducees were more interested in maintaining strong Jewish political posture. They were the rationalists of their day—pragmatic politicians who indulged in Greek logic and forged working relationships with their Roman conquerors. Aristocratic landowners, the Sadducees' power base rested in the priesthood (especially in the office of high priest), which, like land, was connected to ancestral bloodlines. It was in their best interests to maintain the status quo—a people's revolt would only incur Roman wrath, shatter the Jewish society, and ultimately undermine their influence. The radical shift inherent in Jesus' teachings threatened to upset the status quo.

The Sadducees accepted only the Torah's authority. Since Moses made no mention of a resurrection from the dead, they could not accept such a radical and illogical concept.

When it was in their own best interests, the Pharisees and Sadducees joined forces, but each group viewed the affairs of Jewish faith and politics from a profoundly different perspective.

Saul was a Pharisee.

DAMASCUS 3

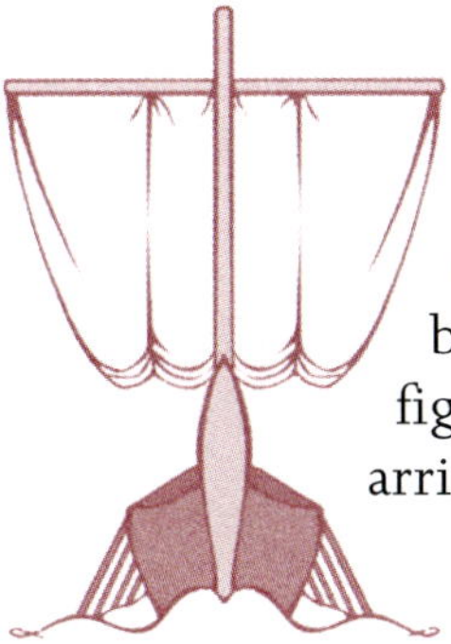

A gasp rippled through the little group of Christians. Mothers instinctively clutched their children closer. Men rose to stand between their families and the unwelcome figure silhouetted in the doorway. Saul had arrived in Damascus.

He entered slowly, his piercing eyes instantly gathering in his surroundings. The worshipers sized him up in return. Saul's bloody reputation as a persecutor of Christians was well known; now the moment of truth had arrived for the group of believers. The opportunity to suffer for Christ was upon them. For a moment there was silence, as if the hunter and each of his prey were facing one another down.

But Saul was not alone. Another man darkened the doorway and entered. It was Ananias, a leader in the church. With raised hand he quieted the confusion. "Brothers and sisters," he said, "you have no reason to fear this man. He has a story to tell."

An unimpressive figure, this mortal enemy of Christians sat down in the midst of the small congregation. In a voice halting and weak, he began to speak.

"I know what you think of me," Saul began. He hesitated. He couldn't quite put his finger on it, but he was sensing something he had never exprienced before. He started over. "Or maybe I don't know what you think of me. But you heard that I was coming to Damascus to do my best to eliminate this movement." Saul paused again. Should he say it? "I had all the authority I needed. Then, three days ago, as I approached your city, something that I still cannot fully understand happened to me. I was suddenly surrounded by an intense, brilliant light that was brighter than the noonday sun. If you think I'm crazy, ask the people who were with me. They saw it too.

"I fell to the ground, dazed. Then a voice spoke to me from the light. 'Saul, Saul, why are you persecuting me?'

"'Who are you, Lord?' I babbled in confusion. But then I saw the one who was talking. It was him; I could not look; his appearance was that brilliant.

"'I am Jesus,' he said, 'the one whom you are persecuting.'

"That's why I'm here today. He told me to come here; I couldn't disobey. 'Get up and go into the city, and you will be told what you must do.' Those were his instructions. Then the vision ended, and I was alone again with my men. But I couldn't see. They had to lead me by the hand. I spent the next three days and nights on my knees, fasting and praying."

"I too had a vision," Ananias interjected. "The Lord told me to go to the house of Judas on Straight Street and find this man. You can imagine how reluctant I was. We all know what the name Saul of Tarsus means to Christians! But who am I to refuse our Lord?"

Saul continued. "On the third day of my fast, in the middle of my darkness, Ananias came to me. He stood beside me and said, 'Brother Saul, receive your sight!' Something like scales fell from my eyes, and suddenly I was able to see. He spoke again: 'And now what are you waiting for? Get up, be baptized, and wash your sins away, calling on his name.'"

The little band of Christians listened carefully. As Saul told his story, the room's tense apprehension had started to melt away.

Then, suddenly, tears welled up in Saul's eyes, and his emotions spilled out in a torrent. Pain and sadness, unspeakable joy and relief—they all gushed out at once, as the once-proud persecutor fell on his knees, sobbing uncontrollably. "I was so wrong! I've caused so much pain and suffering! I've hurt so many people, all because of my blind ignorance, my pride, my arrogance! I persecuted the church of the true and living God! I've slandered Christ, my Lord and my Savior! I have no right to be here." His words gave way to silent weeping.

"This man is now a brother in the Lord," said Ananias quietly. "He has been baptized into the name of Jesus." Turning to Saul, he extended his hand. "The right hand of fellowship," he said. The others quickly gathered around to offer Saul friendship. Their tears flowed freely as they poured out prayers for God's blessings upon the new believer. And Saul now realized what he had sensed when he had entered the room. It was love.

4 A JOURNEY FOR JESUS

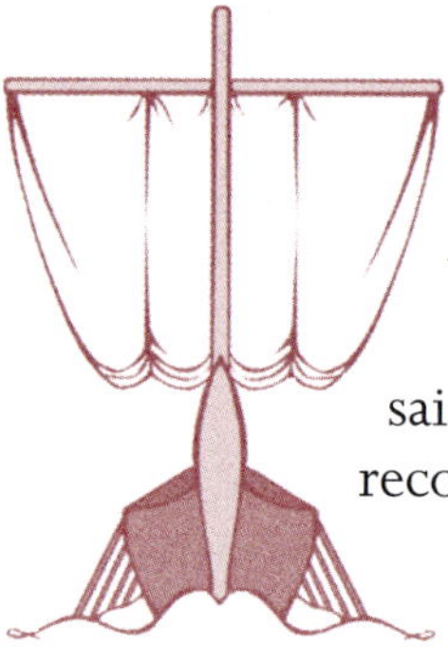

Paul's body shivered uncontrollably. His head felt as if it were on fire; his physical strength was all but gone.

"We have to get him out of Perga," Barnabas said to John Mark, "out of this low country. He'll recover much better in the mountains of Galatia."

"I'm not going up into Galatia," said John Mark. "If that's the direction you're going, then you'll have to go without me. I've had enough anyway!"

It had been several weeks since Paul and the other apostles had left the great city of Antioch in Syria. The Holy Spirit had called them to preach the good news in places where the message of Jesus was unknown. The leaders in the church of Antioch had blessed the apostles and had sent them off on their voyage.

Their first stop had been on the island of Cyprus. After preaching, healing, and driving out demons there, they sailed north toward Asia Minor, disembarking at the port city of Perga. The mosquito-infested lowlands around Perga in Pamphylia were a breeding ground for disease. Exhausted from the difficult journey, Paul had fallen ill. While waiting for Paul to recover, young John Mark had grown impatient. He left for Jerusalem as the other apostles were planning to carry the gospel up into the hills of central Asia Minor.

Paul was still weak, and his vision was still blurry when they left Perga. Nevertheless, he insisted that it was time to press on. As the little band of apostles began the trek inland, Paul fumed at John Mark's departure. "He was too young to come along with us. We never should have brought him."

Barnabas steadied Paul as they continued up the well-traveled road. "Don't dwell on that now," he said. "The important thing is that you recover."

Antioch of Pisidia

In the region of Pisidia, the apostles entered another city called Antioch. On the Sabbath they hurried to the synagogue, eager to share the good news of Christ. As a visiting rabbi, Paul was quickly welcomed into this Jewish community. They invited him to speak to the assembly. Standing up, Paul motioned with his hand and said, "Men of Israel, and you Gentiles who worship God, listen to me." The worshipers listened attentively as Paul recounted the history of the patriarchs and brought to life the Old Testament prophecies. He finished his message with a dramatic conclusion. "We tell you the good news: What God promised our fathers he has fulfilled for us, their children, by raising up Jesus. Therefore, my brothers, I want you to know that through Jesus the forgiveness of sins is proclaimed to you."

The assembly crowded around Paul, anxious to hear more of what the apostle had to say. Soon the whole town was talking about Jesus and his resurrection from the dead. During the next week, Paul and Barnabas preached and taught throughout the community. The next Sabbath they found a full house at the synagogue. It seemed as though the whole region was eager to hear the good news.

But their early success created envy among the Jewish leaders. They began to speak abusively against the things Paul was saying. The same crowd that had welcomed the apostles so warmly now turned against them. Paul and Barnabas suddenly found themselves expelled from the city, leaving behind a small group of spiritually immature disciples.

A pattern had begun to emerge. Each time they entered a town and began to preach at the local synagogue, they would see tremendous initial success. The people were hungry for the truth and eager to hear the good news. But as time went on, the Jews would fall back upon the formal traditions that had been ingrained in them since youth. The self-righteous Jewish leaders would turn the people against Christ and his messengers.

The towns of Galatia

Everywhere the rocky Galatian roads carried them, Paul and Barnabas saw evidence of pagan religions. Temples to Roman and Greek gods crowned the hilltops. At times they could hear the pagan rituals, the late-night revelries, the shouts offered up to mythical gods—gods that could not see or hear, gods of human imagination.

As Paul recovered from his illness, the apostles' steps quickened. In the midst of human darkness, they had the divine light of Christ to share. The task before them was formidable. But the risen Lord was in control—and it was his Word they preached.

In Lystra the townspeople rolled out the red carpet. In pagan fashion the people tried to offer sacrifices to Paul and Barnabas. "The gods have come down to us in human form," they cried. Barnabas they called Zeus, and Paul they named

Hermes. The apostles tore their clothes, pleading with the people not to commit such gross idolatry. When the crowd realized that the missionaries were just mortal men, the mood turned ugly. Paul's thoughts flashed back to another time and place and a stoning he had witnessed—and had celebrated. As the fury of the Lystra mob descended upon him, Paul prayed the same prayer Stephen had prayed. "Lord Jesus, receive my spirit."

A well-aimed rock knocked Paul senseless. Another bounced off his body with a sickening thud. Finally, a few remaining members of the bloodthirsty crowd dragged Paul's limp form outside of the city and left him for dead.

As his head cleared, Paul took inventory of his abused body. He hurt all over, but he was alive. Outside of Lystra, he looked back toward the little Galatian town and collected his thoughts. It had been a rough trip thus far. Could it get worse? He laughed at the irony. "This morning they thought I was a god. In the afternoon they tried to kill me. There's work to be done here," he mused.

Roman Roads

Roman roads were an important element in the rapid spread of the gospel. During the first two centuries A.D., war was relatively infrequent. The Roman caesars kept their troops busy, constructing roads that would eventually serve as the military network that bound the empire together. Such roads were notoriously dangerous for civilians traveling alone. This explains why Paul almost always took companions when he traveled. It also explains why an armed guard escorted Paul, a Roman citizen, when he was being extradited to Rome.

Roman roads were well engineered, shedding water and providing good drainage during the rainy season. In modern times many Roman roads were simply covered by asphalt and are still in use today.

WHICH COVENANT? 5

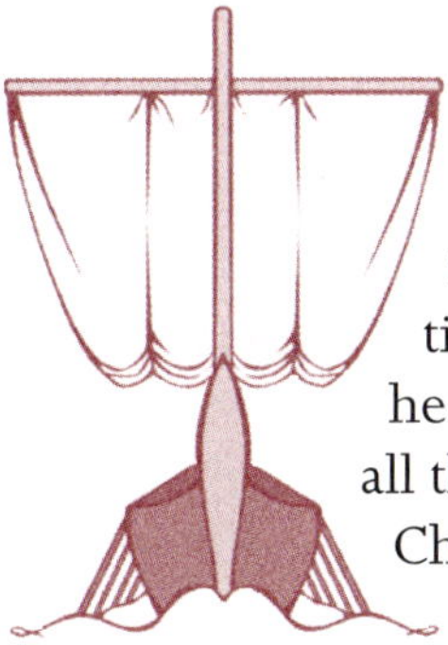

Tempers flared. Angry voices grew louder. The people were taking sides. "What does it mean to be a Christian?" That was the question. Did a person have to become a Jew before he could follow Jesus? Was it necessary to follow all the Jewish rules regarding food and drink? Did Christians still have to worship and rest on the Sabbath? Did males have to be circumcised? The church in Antioch had been growing rapidly; then the problems started. Outsiders had come down from Jerusalem to Antioch. They said, "Unless you are circumcised, according to the custom taught by Moses, you cannot be saved."

Even the apostles were drawn into the controversy. Peter, a leader among the apostles, began to avoid uncircumcised gentile Christians. He should have known better. The Lord had given Peter a vision, showing him that all food was clean to eat and that Gentiles were welcome in the family of God. Peter had even baptized the household of Cornelius, a Gentile. But at this time, Peter worried more about the Jewish leaders than he did about reaching out with Christ's love.

Finally, Paul confronted Peter. He was polite but passionate. Paul reminded his coworker that Jesus had come to call all people to repentance, not just Jews. "We who are Jews by birth and not 'gentile sinners' know that a man is not justified by observing the law but by faith in Jesus Christ. So we too have put our faith in Christ Jesus that we may be justified by faith in Christ and not by observing the law, because by observing the law no one will be justified."

Unfortunately, the seeds of division and mistrust had been sown. Brothers and sisters in Christ now viewed one another with suspicion. Some men, unwilling to undergo circumcision, fell away from Christianity and drifted back into their pagan rituals. Others carried huge burdens on their consciences and were afraid that they weren't really saved.

"We can't have our weak brothers and sisters doubting their salvation in Christ," said Barnabas.

The other leaders in Antioch agreed. "Paul and Barnabas, you will go to Jerusalem."

The Jerusalem Council

James and the other apostles in Jerusalem greeted each ambassador from Antioch with a holy kiss. The leaders of the church rejoiced when they heard how more and more people had come to believe in Jesus as the Savior. But when they heard of the problems in Antioch, their faces darkened.

"This controversy is serious," Peter said. "The men who came from Judea are laying a huge burden on new believers—a yoke that neither we nor our forefathers would have been able to bear. No! We believe it is by the grace of God that Gentiles are saved, just as we are."

Barnabas and Paul chimed in, "The Holy Spirit has been poured out on these gentile believers, just as he was upon us. God has made no distinction between Jews and Gentiles. He has accepted the uncircumcised into his family through faith in Jesus, just as he has accepted us. If only you had seen what we've seen—people of all walks of life filled with the Spirit.

People turning from pagan filth and devoting their lives to Jesus. We've seen amazing signs and wonders!"

Not all were convinced. Some believers who were still members of the Pharisee sect continued to insist, "The Gentiles must be circumcised and required to obey the Law of Moses."

James was silent during most of the discussion. As the half-brother of the Lord Jesus, his words carried tremendous weight. Some people had even noticed a family resemblance to Jesus, and pilgrims to Jerusalem often asked to see James, just to get a glimpse of the Lord's closest living relative. Now all eyes turned to the apostle as he spoke.

"Brothers, listen to me. Simon Peter has described to us how God first gathered the Gentiles unto himself. Therefore, we should not make it difficult for the Gentiles who are turning to God. Instead we should write to them, telling them to abstain from food polluted by idols, from sexual immorality, from the meat of strangled animals, and from blood."

Some of the Jerusalem believers looked shocked. Uncircumcised Gentiles mingling with Jews in the Christian church? But Paul and Barnabas were ecstatic as James confirmed what they had known all along. They were thrilled to be able to carry that letter from Jerusalem back to Antioch. What a comfort it was to be reassured in the truth of salvation by grace alone!

6 OLD FRIENDS, NEW ACQUAINTANCES

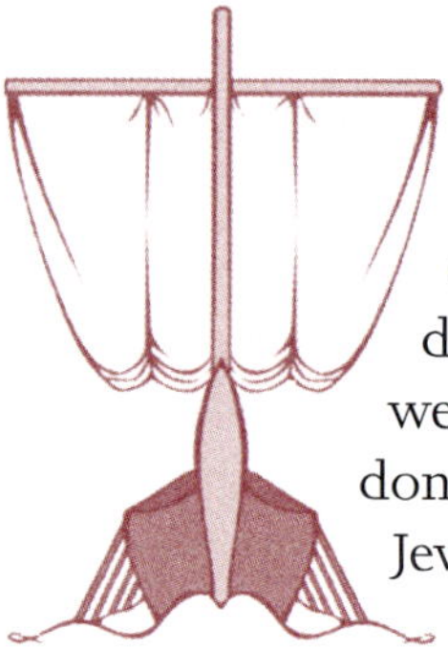

"You don't have to be circumcised to be saved," Paul reminded Timothy. "We're not doing this to fulfill Moses' command. We're doing this so that we don't offend the people we want to serve with the gospel. The Gentiles don't care if you're circumcised or not, but the Jews certainly do. If they learn that you're not circumcised, they won't even let you into the synagogues. They won't let me speak, either, if I associate with an uncircumcised man. We'd never have the chance to introduce them to the Messiah."

Timothy understood perfectly. He winced as the knife sliced through his flesh. Paul grimaced along with his young companion. There was just no way around it: it hurt to get circumcised.

Paul was in Lystra for a second time to encourage the brothers in all the towns where he had preached Christ. Originally he had hoped to bring Barnabas with him, but back in Antioch the two men had butted heads. Barnabas had wanted to bring John Mark along on this journey. Paul, on the other hand, didn't consider the young man reliable since he had abandoned them on their first journey. The disagreement was so sharp that Paul and Barnabas decided to go their separate ways. Paul took Silas with him instead, and Barnabas went back to Cyprus.

Paul remembered Timothy's family from his first visit to Lystra. Timothy's mother, Eunice, was a Jewess. But, because she had married a Greek, she was somewhat of an outcast from the Jewish community. Her son had never been circumcised, and, because the boy was a half-breed, Timothy had never been very welcomed in Jewish company. In spite of her family's second-class status, Eunice had been very careful to teach Timothy everything she could about the Torah. Timothy had known the Scriptures from infancy.

On the other hand, Timothy's family had found a warm welcome among the Christians. Eunice and her family had been baptized into Christ. Timothy, always eager to learn, had quickly grasped the truths of the Christian faith. His sharp mind and outgoing personality had caught Paul's eye. Paul knew that the lad's gifts could be useful in the church. Paul saw this journey as an opportunity for Timothy to grow as a leader.

It took a few days for Timothy's wound to heal. Paul used the time to strengthen the believers in Lystra. It had been only a few years since he and Barnabas had come through the little town, but the climate had changed considerably since the apostles' first visit. The little group of Christians had grown. The Jews still tried to stir up trouble for the believers whenever possible, but usually they found little support among the townspeople. The pagans just wanted to live and let live, and they had little use for religious squabbling.

When the time finally came for Paul, Timothy, and the others to leave, they paused to reflect on the town that had once almost taken Paul's life. Some of the stones strewn about still looked familiar. There was a smile on Paul's face as he turned toward the west and set Lystra behind him for a second time. How things had changed! God's word had borne fruit.

OLD FRIENDS, NEW ACQUAINTANCES

A new companion and a new call

The apostles revisited all the towns of Galatia, encouraging believers as they went. They carried the letter from the Jerusalem council which affirmed that Gentiles and Jews were one family through faith in Christ. Troublemakers still tried to force the Galatian Christians to turn back to the Law of Moses, but the churches stood firm in their Christian freedom.

Now God had a new direction for the missionaries. The Spirit of Jesus kept leading them farther and farther west, down to the sea. Finally they came to the western end of Asia Minor, where they rested in the city of Troas.

In Troas, Paul and Timothy met a Gentile named Luke. Luke was an educated man, a doctor who had been trained in the best tradition of the Greek physician Hippocrates. Luke had only recently come to faith in Christ, and now he was on fire for Jesus. His passion to tell others about Jesus made a strong impression on Paul.

Luke had already begun to write the story of the fledgling Christian church, starting with Jesus' ascension from the Mount of Olives, the exciting events of Pentecost, and the spread of the good news out of Judea and into the world. Now he busily scribbled notes as he listened to Paul telling about the apostles' travels through Galatia.

Paul had a proposal for the good doctor. "I want you to join us," Paul urged Luke. "You have a love for lost souls. I know you want to reach the Gentiles with the message of Christ. Why don't you continue the journey with us? You can chronicle our travels, so that others can hear of the great things God is doing among the unbelieving.

"There's only one thing," cautioned Paul. "I don't know exactly where we're going. I thought we would go to Asia or Bithynia, but the Spirit of Jesus has prevented us. God has led us here to Troas, and he will lead us on from here."

Paul lay awake long after the lamps had been extinguished. He thought of the believers back in Antioch in Syria who had sent him out in the name of the Lord to preach the good news. He thought of the elders in Lystra, Derbe, Iconium, and all the other towns scattered throughout the hills of Galatia. He thought of Timothy's mother, Eunice, and his grandmother, Lois. "They're all praying for me," he remembered. It was a comforting thought. "No matter where the Lord leads us, God's people are praying that our message will take root and all will be saved and come to a knowledge of the truth."

Then, as Paul continued to meditate, the darkness of the room gave way to a soft glow. An image appeared. Paul rubbed his eyes. Was he dreaming? No, a man—a Greek man—stood before him, beckoning to Paul, pleading with him, "Come over and help us!" Then, as quickly as he had appeared, the man vanished.

It took Paul only a moment to grasp what he had seen. Here was an urgent call from the Lord—a call to visit a new continent. Quickly he roused Silas, Timothy, and Luke and told them of the vision he had just seen. "The Lord has spoken," he said. "We're going to preach Christ where he has never been preached before. We're going to Macedonia."

7 THE FIRST CHRISTIANS IN MACEDONIA

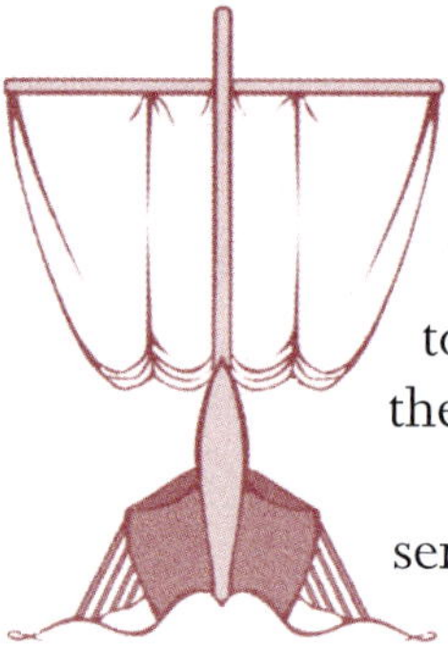

The journey from Troas had been quick, almost frantic. Paul, Silas, Timothy, and Luke boarded a ship for the short trip across the sea to Samothrace, then to Neapolis, and finally to the Macedonian city of Philippi.

Philippi had a distinctly Roman flavor. Rome sent its retired army veterans there to live out their days in peace and quiet.

Outside the city gate, a group of women had gathered under the trees for prayer. One of them introduced herself to Paul and his companions as Lydia, a dealer in purple cloth. She was a worshiper of the true God, and now the Lord opened her heart to respond to Paul's message about the Savior.

"I want to be baptized into Christ," she pleaded. "I, and my household."

The apostles were overwhelmed as they saw God's Holy Spirit at work. As it had happened many times before, they witnessed God's grace in action as another child of God was reborn into Christ. "Lydia, I baptize you in the name of the Father and of the Son and of the Holy Spirit," Paul said as he applied water from the stream. Simple water joined with the power of God's Word gave this woman and her family new identities in God's family. There was hardly a dry eye in the little crowd that had gathered beside the river.

In jail for Jesus

The joy was short lived. A pesky slave woman began following the apostles around Philippi. The woman was demon possessed and had earned a lot of money for her owners by telling the future. Everywhere the apostles went the woman screamed at the crowds that followed, "These men are servants of the Most High God, who are telling you the way to be saved." What she said was, of course, true, but her announcement frustrated the message Paul and Silas shared.

Finally, when Paul could tolerate the woman's screaming no longer, he addressed the unclean spirit who possessed her: "In the name of Jesus Christ I command you to come out of her!" Immediately the demon left the woman, and she was restored to her right mind. The crowds were amazed. The slave woman's owners were furious.

"These men are Jews who are advocating unlawful customs!" the owners cried to the city magistrates. The crowd joined in, and in short order the missionaries found themselves surrounded by a hostile mob.

The burly Roman soldiers were rough when they seized the apostles. At the command of the magistrates, Paul and Silas were stripped and beaten. The apostles gritted their teeth as blow after blow of the Roman whips shredded their skin. Now they knew how their Lord Jesus felt before Pilate.

The inner dungeon was a disgusting place. The smell of human urine and excrement permeated even the walls. Rats scurried underfoot. From somewhere in the darkness came the agonized groan of another prisoner who shared their painful lot.

"Give thanks to the Lord, for he is good. His love endures forever!" The words of the great psalm came spontaneously from Paul's and Silas' lips. The Romans could break their bodies, but their unbroken spirits were still filled with joy. The moans of the other prisoners grew silent. The melodies of the psalms and hymns echoed through the dank chambers of the dungeon. Prayers cascaded through the passageways, filling the prison with sounds never before heard there.

Suddenly there was a lurch. A shock wave rumbled through the cells, down the hallways, shaking the prison to its very foundation. The whole building moved. Guards were thrown from their feet like rag dolls and hurled against the walls. Earthquake!

For the prisoners, fear gave way to amazement. Instead of finding themselves buried under mountains of rubble, they watched as the cell doors miraculously burst open. The stocks that had bound them rattled open. They were free! One by one the prisoners picked their way through the dust and debris.

As the air cleared, Paul saw something that caused him to leap into action. "Wait! Don't do it!" he screamed. The head jailer held a short Roman sword in his right hand. Earthquake or not, he knew what happened to jailers who let their prisoners escape. Better to finish his life quickly himself than to face a slow, agonizing death at the hands of his Roman masters. The man had gathered up his tunic to expose his chest. He was about to plunge the sword deep into his belly to end his life.

"Don't harm yourself! We're all still here!" Paul shouted.

The jailer looked on in amazement at the motley group of bruised, crusty, unshaven men standing before him in the torchlight. None of his prisoners had run away. Trembling with relief and gratitude, he fell at their feet. He felt like kissing their feet, but there was a pressing question on his mind for these two who were servants of God. How could they be so filled with joy under such miserable circumstances? What power their god must have to send an earthquake just to free them! The jailer knew the question he had to ask. "Sirs," he said with deep respect, "what must I do to be saved?"

Without hesitation the apostles replied, "Believe in the Lord Jesus, and you will be saved—you and your household."

Later that night, in the jailer's living quarters, Paul and Silas told of God's love in sending Jesus. They spoke of the forgiveness of sins, of the release from guilt. They shared the good news of real freedom from the shackles of sin and death. The jailer and his family listened, wide-eyed, as they heard how the only Son of God had died for them, rose again, and was now preparing a place for them in heaven.

One by one, each member of the jailer's family—from the eldest to the very youngest—received the washing of Holy Baptism. With joy in their hearts, the whole family shared a late-night feast with the apostles. Their new lives in Christ had to be celebrated.

8 THE WISDOM OF MEN OR THE FOOLISHNESS OF CHRIST?

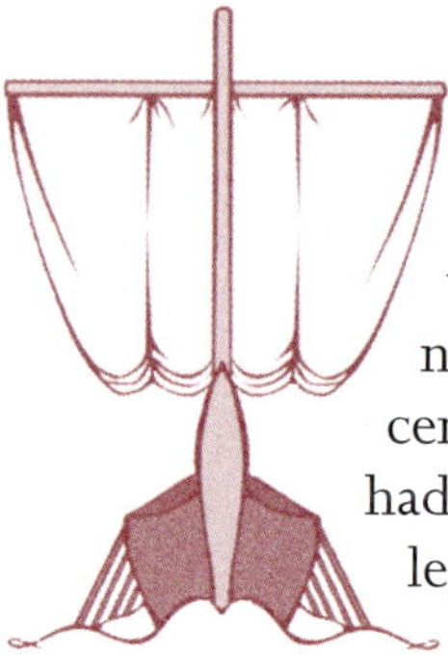

The Athenian intellectuals stood around all day at the gathering place on Mars Hill and bantered about ideas. Each fancied himself a worthy debater. Each imagined himself as the next Aristotle or Plato or Socrates. Though several centuries had passed since the great philosophers had taught in these courtyards, their philosophical legacies were legendary.

Paul saw through the charade. These aspiring men of Athens were only dreamers. Their intellectual abilities were pathetic. They were fools, really—merely human philosophers constantly in search of wisdom and always coming up short. The city of Athens was full of such nonsense.

"Men of Athens, I see that you are in every way very religious," Paul began. He played to the images they had of themselves. "For as I walked around and looked at your objects of worship, I even found an altar with this inscription: TO AN UNKNOWN GOD. Now what you worship as something unknown, I am going to proclaim to you.

"The God who made the world and everything in it is the Lord of heaven and earth and does not live in temples built by human hands. We should not think that the divine being is like gold or silver or stone—an image made by man's desire and skill. In the past God overlooked such ignorance, but now he commands all people everywhere to repent. For he has set a day when he will judge the world with justice through the man he has appointed. He has given proof of this to all men by raising this man from the dead."

"What's this babbler trying to say?" sneered some of the philosophers standing nearby. "He seems to be advocating foreign gods. And what's this about resurrection from the dead?" Every Greek philosopher knew that the whole purpose of good living was to escape the body, not to have your body raised back from the dead so that you could live forever.

But others were fascinated by what Paul had to say: One God instead of many gods who quarreled like spoiled children. Eternal life in paradise instead of a perpetual existence in the land of shadows. Real life with Christ now and for all eternity instead of empty philosophies that offered no comfort. The Spirit called some to faith through the divine foolishness of Christ crucified.

Life on the wild side

The city of Corinth was quite another matter. It was a natural stopping place for men of the sea who reveled in the raucous life found in a port of call. Corinth was situated on a narrow strip of land that joined northern and southern Greece. From the Aegean Sea east of town, it was only a short distance across the isthmus to the Adriatic Sea on the west. Enterprising Corinthian engineers had built an intriguing little railway that connected the two bodies of water. Ships and their cargo were pulled up out of the water onto the tracks and hauled overland to the other side. The overland haul was quicker and much safer than navigating the treacherous waters along the shores of southern Greece. While their ships and cargo were being moved, the bars and brothels of Corinth invited sailors to sample their wares. The word *Corinthian* had become synonymous with life in a moral cesspool.

As Paul surveyed the city, he couldn't help but wonder, "What fruits would the gospel bear here? Would a call to repentance in such an immoral place have any effect at all?" Perhaps they should pass through the city in search of mission fields that offered more promise. Still, the Corinthians needed a Savior too. If the light of Christ could shine here, it could shine anywhere, for there was certainly no shortage of sinners.

Timothy and Silas had stayed in Macedonia, leaving Paul feeling very alone and out of his element. While he anticipated little return on his patient investment of time and energy, he was surprised to discover that it didn't take long for him to make a connection. A man named Aquila—a fellow Jew—took Paul under his wing and invited him to stay at his home.

"How did you come to live in this wretched place?" Paul asked his newfound acquaintance.

"It's a long story," Aquila replied. "Originally I'm from Pontus. Then I lived in Rome for a time. I'm a tentmaker, just as you are. I was making a good living, but a persecution broke out against Jews in Rome. Claudius Caesar ordered all Jews out of the city, so my wife, Priscilla, and I came here. It's been tough starting over, and the moral climate is not good for my family. But we've done all right. The Jewish community is close-knit here; we stick together."

Aquila was impressed by Paul's tent-making skills. Paul had been a master craftsman, learning his trade well in Tarsus. Between the many pilgrims visiting the pagan shrines and the people who came to Corinth to visit the Isthmian games, the two men found a ready market for their tents. They worked together well and learned from each other as they waited for Silas and Timothy to rejoin them.

Through Aquila's influence, Paul found an open door to preaching to the Jewish community. Every Sabbath, Paul seized the opportunity to talk about Christ crucified to anyone in the synagogue who would listen. "Look at the prophecies!" he would say. "Jesus was born of a virgin, just as Isaiah had said. He was born in Bethlehem, in fulfillment of the words of Micah. Isaiah described Jesus' suffering and death as vividly as if he had been at the foot of the cross. David's psalms paint such a clear picture of the Messiah—and they're all fulfilled in Jesus. Look at the evidence! Don't put your trust in obedience to the law; the law can't save you. Trust in Jesus, your Savior and the Savior of the world."

A double effect

As he saw the effect of the gospel, Paul remembered the words of Jesus, "I have not come to bring peace, but a sword." He saw that happening in Corinth. The synagogue was divided. Some became passionate disciples of Christ. Others fiercely opposed the message of Jesus.

Sometimes Paul felt as if he was getting nowhere, but the Word of the Lord encouraged him to continue. "Do not be afraid; keep on speaking and do not be silent," the Lord said to him in a vision. "I am with you. No one is going to attack and harm you, because I have many people in this city."

WISDOM OR FOOLISHNESS?

Paul stayed in Corinth for a year and a half. It was the longest he had stayed in any city during his travels. Paul grew to feel a special affection for the believers in Corinth—that personal bond of a pastor with his people. They were a divisive lot, to be sure, always arguing among themselves. Paul had to be gentle with them as he taught them how to live free in Christ. The gentile believers, on the other hand, had trouble separating themselves from the pagan culture in which they had grown up. It would take time for them to grow and learn the obedience that comes from faith. They were still learning that God's grace was not to be abused in carnal living and that Christian liberty was not a license for continued immorality.

Paul and his companions spent enough time in Corinth to see the little congregation of Christians begin to blossom and bear fruit. Jews and Gentiles studied the Scriptures together, and their faith grew and matured. The arguments became less frequent, and the divisions slowly began to heal.

As the boat carried them slowly out of the Corinthian harbor, Paul, Silas, and Timothy reminisced about their experiences in Greece. "Jews demand miraculous signs, and Greeks look for wisdom, but we preach Christ crucified: a stumbling block to Jews and foolishness to Gentiles. But to those whom God has called, both Jews and Greeks, Christ is the power and wisdom of God." All the arguments and reasoning of human wisdom were nothing compared to God's power. And only because of him could believers be found in this filthy city—only because of him.

PEACE IN EPHESUS 9

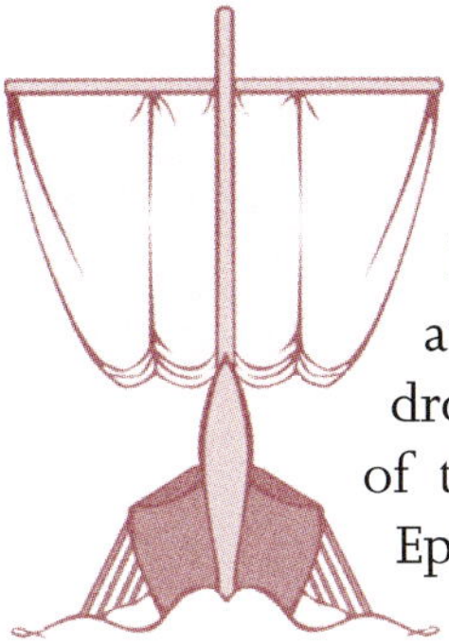

Dry stubble covered the hills around Ephesus. It had been months since the parched ground had seen rain. Here and there a few emaciated goats tried to find something to eat. The drought had devastated the whole eastern end of the Mediterranean. But what seemed bad in Ephesus was nothing compared to the famine farther east. A Christian man returning from Jerusalem reported, "The believers in Jerusalem are starving. There is hardly any food to be found in the city. And the Jews are doing their best to keep Christians from getting what little there is."

"Then we have a wonderful opportunity to serve our brothers and sisters in the faith," said Paul. "Let's gather an offering from all the churches in this region. I'll personally carry it to Jerusalem to help alleviate the suffering."

Paul spent nearly three years in Ephesus. During that time the Word of the Lord had produced results beyond the apostles' wildest dreams. Every day Paul had preached in the lecture hall of Tyrannus so that all the Jews and Greeks in the area could hear the gospel. Former sorcerers had turned away from Satan and now followed the Lord Jesus. They had brought all their scrolls of demonic rituals and incantations and had publicly burned them in a bonfire. The thriving mother church in Ephesus had spun off daughter congregations at Philadelphia, Smyrna, and other cities. While the hills around Ephesus were thirsty for rain, the thirst of God's people had been quenched with the living water of Christ.

PEACE IN EPHESUS

Trouble in Corinth

The report of the famine in Jerusalem wasn't the only troubling news Paul received while in Ephesus. Sadly, the congregation in Corinth was back at it again. Rumor was that there were quarrels, immorality, lawsuits, and abuses at the Lord's Table. What a mess! It was exasperating. But it had to be dealt with. Paul prayed for inspiration from on high as he penned his letter.

"I always thank God for you because of his grace given you in Christ Jesus," Paul began. It was true. He loved those weak, ignorant, carnal troublemakers so deeply. Sometimes he felt like embracing them, at other times he felt like he needed to give them a good thrashing. After all the time he had spent with them, didn't they know better? "Don't you know that you yourselves are God's temples and that God's Spirit lives in you? Don't you know that a little yeast works through the whole batch of dough? Get rid of the old yeast that you may be a new batch without yeast—as you really are.

"Do you not know that the saints will judge the world? Do you not know that the wicked will not inherit the kingdom of God? But you were washed, you were sanctified, you were justified in the name of the Lord Jesus Christ and by the Spirit of our God.

"Do you not know that he who unites himself with a prostitute is one with her in body? You are not your own. You were bought at a price. Therefore, honor God with your body.

"Do you not know that in a race all the runners run, but

only one gets the prize? Run in such a way as to get the prize!"

As Paul made the rounds to gather an offering for the saints in Jerusalem, he realized he was going to have to spend some more time in Corinth.

To Jerusalem with love

The drought had taken its toll everywhere. The believers at Philippi were experiencing extreme hardship, but they pleaded with Paul for the privilege of contributing to the offering for Jerusalem. The Corinthians needed more persuading, but they had grown tremendously from Paul's letters, and they too stepped up to meet the challenge.

Soon Paul and his group found themselves carrying a substantial amount of money. But it wasn't the money that mattered. The coins in the strongbox were just evidence of the believers' deep devotion to the Lord Jesus. They knew the grace of the Lord Jesus Christ—that though he was rich, yet for their sakes he had become poor, so that they, through his poverty, could become rich in spiritual things. Money couldn't buy peace, but God had given all these Christians the peace that passes all understanding.

Before heading for Jerusalem, Paul and his companions stopped once more near Ephesus. It always brought such joy to Paul's heart to see how God's Word had spread in these parts. The elders of the church met him at Miletus, bringing their own gift for the saints in Jerusalem.

Paul felt a deep attachment to these Christians to whom he had given three years of his life. His words were charged with emotion as he spoke. "I'm going to Jerusalem, not knowing what will happen to me there. I only know that in every city the Holy Spirit warns me that I am facing imprisonment and hardships. However, I consider my life worth nothing to me, if only I may finish the race and complete the task the Lord Jesus has given me—the task of testifying to the gospel of God's grace."

The elders listened intently as Paul gave them a solemn charge, "Keep watch over yourselves and all the flock of which the Holy Spirit has made you overseers. Be shepherds of the church of God, which he bought with his blood."

The believers gathered around to pray. They embraced Paul and kissed him. They waved from the pier as his tiny ship pulled away from shore, tearful at the apostles' departure, but filled with joy at their service to the saints. Though great distances would separate them, Paul and the Ephesians would always be united by the bond of peace. And they would meet again in heaven.

THE RIGHTS OF A ROMAN 10

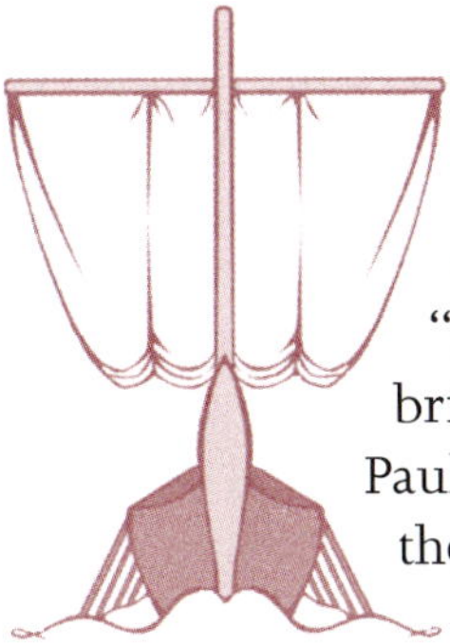

"It's him!" The men at the temple in Jerusalem pointed at Paul. "Look, it's the one who teaches against our law," they shouted. "See, he has even defiled this holy place by bringing Greeks into the temple area." Seizing Paul, they dragged him out of the temple. While they were getting ready to kill him, news reached the commander of the Roman troops.

Paul actually sighed with relief when the Roman soldiers came to arrest him. Roman chains were better than getting beaten to death by a Jewish mob. But the rioters tried to reach past the soldiers to get at Paul. The soldiers had to carry Paul because of the violence.

"May I say something to you?" Paul pleaded with the commander.

"Do you speak Greek?" he asked. "Aren't you the Egyptian who started a revolt and led four thousand terrorists out into the desert some time ago?"

"No, sir," Paul answered. "I am a Jew, from Tarsus in Cilicia. Please let me speak to the people."

With the commander's permission, Paul motioned to the crowd. The mob grew silent when they heard Paul speak to them in Aramaic, their own language. He told them of his days as a persecutor, how he had never known any peace in his life until that fateful day on the road to Damascus. "Under Gamaliel I was thoroughly trained in the law of our fathers and was just as zealous for God as any of you are today. I persecuted the followers of the Way to their deaths, arresting both men and women and throwing them into prison," he said. "When the blood of Stephen was shed, I stood there giving my approval. But the Lord Jesus changed my life, and God gave me a commission: 'Go; I will send you far away to preach to the Gentiles.'"

Until now the crowd had listened intently but, at the mention of the Gentiles, the rioting started again. "Rid the earth of him! He's not fit to live!" they shouted. The Jews started throwing off their cloaks and flinging dust into the air.

"Take him inside the barracks," ordered the commander. "Flog him until he talks. Find out what he's done to turn this whole city upside down." The centurion followed orders and prepared to flog Paul.

"Is it legal for you to flog a Roman citizen who hasn't been found guilty?" Paul asked the centurion.

The centurion's eyes grew wide. He called immediately for the commander. "What are you going to do?" he asked his superior. "This man is a Roman citizen."

Rushing back, the commander asked Paul, "Are you a Roman citizen?"

"I was born a citizen," Paul replied. He emphasized the word "born" just enough to get the point across. He knew he had the full attention of the commander. He would receive better treatment from now on.

From Caesarea to Caesar

Jerusalem was no longer a safe place for Paul. Too many people remembered him as a Pharisee who once hated

Christians. Now they weren't sure if they could trust him. In an effort to resolve the case, the Roman command ordered Paul to stand before the Jewish ruling council. But that resolved nothing and only caused more arguing among the Jews.

Paul had said to the Sanhedrin, "My brothers, I am a Pharisee—the son of a Pharisee. I stand on trial because of my hope in the resurrection of the dead." The Pharisees, who believed in the resurrection, took sides with Paul. The Sadducees, on the other hand, vigorously opposed him.

The commander saw that the situation was about to turn violent, with Paul caught in the middle. When the Romans learned of a plot against Paul's life, the commander decided it was time to take action.

Paul couldn't help thinking, "This is impressive. Citizenship has its privileges." He was surrounded by a detachment of Roman soldiers—200 infantrymen, 70 horsemen, and 200 spearmen. His escort took him safely out of Jerusalem to the palace of Governor Felix in the city of Caesarea.

Paul's trip to Jerusalem had accomplished its purpose. Before his arrest he had been able to deliver the gift from the churches. The offering had been well received, and some of the hardships among the Jerusalem believers had eased. Paul had a chance to speak to the Jews in Jerusalem about their Savior—and to the Sanhedrin, no less. Now the Holy Spirit confirmed Paul's new direction: "Take courage! As you have testified about me in Jerusalem, so you must also testify in Rome."

When he arrived in Caesarea, Paul looked at every situation as an opportunity to tell the story of God's grace in

Christ. He thought of Jesus' words, "On my account you will be brought before governors and kings as witnesses to them and to the Gentiles. When they arrest you, do not worry about what to say or how to say it. At that time you will be given words to say." Paul witnessed to anyone who would listen. He talked of righteousness, self-control, and the judgment to come. He spoke to the lowest levels of society and the highest government officials in the province—even to Governor Felix and to Porcius Festus, who succeeded him.

But Paul's case was beginning to drag out. Felix wanted to curry favor with the Jews by keeping Paul on a short leash. He hoped Paul might offer him a bribe in exchange for freedom. Festus wanted to send Paul back to Jerusalem—and certain death.

Finally, there was really no other place to turn. "If the charges brought against me by these Jews are not true, no one has the right to hand me over to them," asserted Paul in his own defense. "I appeal to Caesar!"

"Very well then," said Governor Festus. "You have appealed to Caesar. To Caesar you will go."

Roman Law

The authority of Roman law extended to commerce, slave ownership, common law property, and the rights and privileges of Roman citizenship.

In the first Christian century, nearly half of the Roman Empire consisted of slaves. Under Roman law an owner had total authority over his slaves. On the other hand, Roman law also permitted intercession on behalf of a condemned slave. Whenever possible, the early Christians worked through the Roman legal system to help slaves attain earthly freedom. The story of Onesimus and Philemon, and the apostle Paul's intervention in this relationship, probably did more to overcome slavery than any other documented case in history. The slave theme echoes throughout the New Testament, a metaphor for spiritual enslavement in sin and our new freedom in Christ's death and resurrection.

Roman law was also instrumental in securing a trial for the apostle Paul. All Roman citizens could claim this right, complete with an official hearing before the legitimate ruling authority of jurisdiction. Paul's citizenship also saved him from a torturous end, mercifully prohibiting his crucifixion. Roman citizens were instead given the dignity of being executed by decapitation.

Passage by Sea

Paul probably booked passage on beamy, slow-moving merchant ships. The larger ones could be up to 180 feet in length and carry 1,200 tons, plus passengers and crew. These ships would sail along a coastline waiting for favorable winds before striking out in open water. Driven by a large square sail on a central mast, they would also carry many oars for those times when winds were unfavorable. The larger vessels might also have a second small foresail sloping forward, more for control than drive.

Ships of this type were hard to maneuver. By bracing the sails, they could, however, sail within eight degrees of the wind, making tacking less necessary.

Two large oars lashed to the stern usually served as rudders. These could be fixed in a permanent position in bad weather. The weather hazard dreaded most was an overcast sky because it made navigation by the stars virtually impossible.

11 ALL ROADS LEAD TO ROME

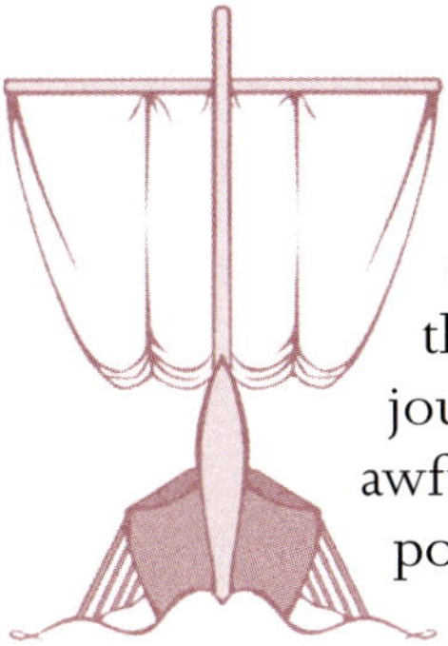

The voyage had been terrible. It wasn't just that Paul was being deprived of liberty for crimes he had never committed. It wasn't just that he had been chained for much of the journey. The late autumn weather had been awful. The sea had been rough. They had been pounded for weeks by gale forces that swept across the sea. Their ship had been battered to pieces, and the hapless passengers and crew had been washed ashore like driftwood.

But, after three months wintering on the island of Malta, they were safe! Paul was thankful that he had Luke, a physician, along. Not only had Luke been able to attend to the injuries of the shipwreck victims, he had been an invaluable companion all around, carefully chronicling everything that had happened.

As the apostle walked along the Via Appia ahead of the centurion who was guarding him, Paul felt the weight of his years bearing down on him. This hadn't been his first shipwreck. And how often had he been accused and arrested, flogged or imprisoned! How often he had been close to death for the sake of the gospel! But he wasn't a young man anymore. His body was tired. He had only one great task that still had to be completed.

The sight of the capital lifted Paul's spirits. The great city of Rome stood before Paul and his companions. Sprawled across seven hills, the city's public buildings gleamed in the bright sunlight of spring. The Roman Forum, the Senate, the residence of the emperor—things that Paul had heard about for years but had never seen. Now they invited him to enter and tell his story. Here he would testify before Caesar of a greater kingdom ruled by an even greater king.

Onesimus and Philemon

Even if Paul was bound by chains, he was permitted a certain amount of freedom. For two years he lived in his own rented house with only a soldier to guard him. Christians from different parts of the empire stopped to visit. The believers in Rome made sure that all his material needs were met.

As always, Paul used every opportunity to preach Christ. He moved with ease among the Roman upper classes. He even found an audience among some of the members of Caesar's own household. He waited for the day when he would be permitted to testify before the emperor himself.

"Onesimus? Is that you?" Paul and Timothy recognized the young man from Colosse. The boy had been a slave in that city near Ephesus and had belonged to a believer named Philemon. Onesimus had run away from his master and had come to Rome to seek his fortune in the capital. Here he could disappear among the labyrinthine streets of the sprawling city. But it was more than just a chance acquaintance that brought the young man and Paul together. It was the Lord's plan.

Young Onesimus was tired of running. So much guilt! So much fear! He had lived looking over his shoulder long enough. There had been a time, earlier in his life, when he had heard Paul speak back in Colosse, but he had not been interested in the apostle's message. Now the seed of the gospel had been planted and had taken root. Now the Holy Spirit was ready to produce the fruits of repentance and faith.

The new believer served Paul as faithfully as any of the apostle's other companions—perhaps more so. Onesimus became like a son to Paul, a dear companion to him in his hours of need. But both Paul and Onesimus knew what had to be done. Paul wrote a letter to Philemon, urging Onesimus' master to take him back—no longer as a slave, but as a brother in the Lord.

Paul felt as if he were losing part of his heart as he bade farewell to Onesimus. Both had tears in their eyes as Onesimus began the long journey from Rome back to the place where he rightly belonged.

It wasn't hard to keep busy while waiting for his chance to testify before Caesar. Paul kept up a lively correspondence with the churches he had started. He remembered the exciting years at Ephesus, where the gospel had spread so quickly, and the Philippians, who even in their hardship gave so generously. Even if Paul was in prison, God's Word could never be chained!

The verdict

Finally the day came. Paul was ushered into the throne room to testify before Caesar.

Surrounded by familiar faces, Paul actually felt quite at ease. He knew most of the members of the Palace Guard. They, in turn, knew that he was in chains for Christ. Some of the members of Caesar's household were there too, secretly praying on Paul's behalf.

Emperor Nero—a man of deep suspicions—was the last survivor in an imperial family whose bloodline had deteriorated with each succeeding generation. Some said it was the water the emperor's family drank. Others whispered about inbreeding. These days there was a lot of whispering going on around Caesar's palace, and the emperor didn't like it. He imagined plots and coups, even among his closest advisers and family members.

Paul addressed the emperor with deep respect. But he wouldn't give in to the pagan custom of worshiping the emperor as a god. Ever since Octavian had taken the title "Augustus" a century earlier, Roman emperors had demanded divine worship. A pinch of incense or a drink offering was all that was required, but it was more than any Christian was willing to give.

It was hard to tell what the outcome would be. The expression on Caesar's face changed as Paul testified. Nero seemed to listen thoughtfully as Paul told of the life and death of Jesus. He looked mildly amused when Paul spoke of the crucified Jesus returning to life on the third day—crucifixion was not something people came back from. As Paul spoke of repentance and faith and obedience to the will of God, Nero's face hardened. The emperor's immoral proclivities were well-known throughout the palace.

"The man is innocent. He is to be set free." With a wave of his hand, Nero Caesar dismissed the court. The prisoner's story was cute but hardly worth a great emperor's time. The verdict was almost anticlimactic. After all the waiting and anticipating, Paul was a free man!

"What are you going to do now?" Timothy asked Paul.

"As long as the Lord gives me strength, I'm going to continue preaching the gospel," Paul answered. "I've always wanted to preach the good news where it's never been preached before. Maybe now I'll finally get to Spain."

12 POURED OUT LIKE A DRINK OFFERING

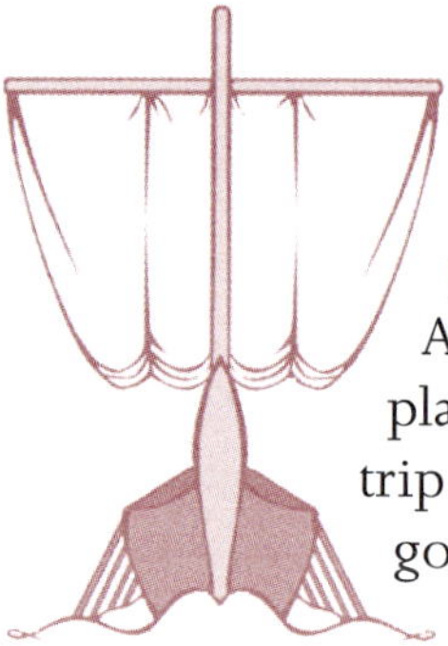

The old man shivered in the cold prison cell. He thought of how his advancing years hadn't prevented him from traveling and preaching. After Caesar had set him free, Paul had visited places he could only have dreamed of before. His trip to Spain had taken him as far west as he could go. Back at Ephesus he had worked for a short time with Timothy, but his passion to reach more unbelievers drove him to move on.

The mood in Rome had turned ugly since Paul's last imprisonment. A huge fire had destroyed much of Rome, and Nero, always paranoid, had made the Christians the scapegoats for his vengeance. Christians throughout the city were being swept up in the persecution. Even Peter had been taken into custody in Rome.

Paul felt very alone. He wished that John Mark could be with him. Ah, yes, John Mark, the young man who had abandoned the work on the first journey through Perga. That was long ago. Paul and John Mark had long since reconciled, and Paul had come to appreciate John Mark's maturity.

Now only Luke remained with the apostle. All the others were gone. Paul turned to the Lord Jesus. "I know in whom I have believed," Paul wrote to Timothy, "and am convinced that he is able to guard what I have entrusted to him. I am already being poured out like a drink offering, and the time has come for my departure. I have fought the good fight. I have finished the race. I have kept the faith. Now there is in store for me the crown of righteousness, which the Lord, the righteous judge, will award to me on that day—and not only to me, but to all those who have longed for his appearing."

The prisoner berated himself for leaving behind his precious scrolls back in Troas. It would have been so comforting for him to have been able to immerse himself in God's Word. Instead he would have to rely on his memory for passages from Scripture that he had known since his childhood in Tarsus—passages that he had so often shared with others, passages that brought him so much peace.

"Do your best to come to me quickly," he pleaded in his letter to Timothy. "When you come, bring the cloak that I left with Carpus at Troas, and my scrolls, especially the parchments. Do your best to get here before winter."

There was no fanfare when the executioner came. As a Roman citizen, Paul would not be crucified or burned at the stake or devoured by wild animals. Unlike the slow, painful death of his Lord Jesus on the cross, Paul's departure would be mercifully swift, almost painless. He remembered the words the Holy Spirit had given him to write to the Philippians, "For to me to live is Christ, and to die is gain."

The sword flashed. The victim's severed head fell from his body. Saint Paul of Tarsus, apostle to the Gentiles and martyr, had given up his life for Christ.